TOLEDO CATHEDRAL

History and Art

Text:
Luís Alba González

Translated by:
David Fricker.

Text:
D. Luis Alba González.

Translated by:
David Fricker

Exclusive Distribution:
© Julio de la Cruz
C/ Ciudad, 3
45002 Toledo
Tel. 925 – 22.28.09

Printed in Spain by Artes Gráficas Toledo, S.A.U.
I.S.B.N.: 84-87318-13-4
D.L. TO: 605-2004

Photography: **F. Garrido**, Oronoz, Foima, Manipel and José Ramón Martín.

INTRODUCTION

Dear Reader,

You hold in your hands a short guide to Toledo cathedral. This is not just one more cathedral, like those you have already visited, but the most important monument and museum of the City of Toledo. It is in itself a summary and compendium of the art, traditions and legends of this magical city.

This book mainly describes what is normally on view, although it does contain additional information on places which are more difficult to visit.

There is a popular saying which, in several different forms, describes the cathedral together with several of its sisters: «Pulchra Leonina, Fortis Abulensis, Dives Toletana, Sancta Ovetensis»: Leon cathedral is pure, Avila's is strong, Toledo cathedral is rich and that of Oviedo is Holy.

Cathedral facade

THE ENTRANCE TO THE CATHEDRAL

The normal way in is through the only door giving direct access to the Cloisters from the street.

Style: this is Gothic, Toledo cathedral being the second one in Spain built in this style, after the first, at Seville. The inside lengths of both, like many others of the greatest churches in the world, are shown within the Basilica of Saint Peter, in Rome. The best overall view is that from the foot of the nave. However, the Choir blocks what would otherwise be the magnificent complete view of the inside as a whole. This is the case with the majority of Spanish cathedrals.

The first stone of the cathedral was laid by the king of Castile and Leon, Fernando III, in 1226. He was accompanied in this by the archbishop and great promotor of the work, Jiménez de Rada, who was from Navarre. Construction of the cathedral lasted until 1493.

Once again, the importance of this building is shown by a folk saying: Seville is the box, Toledo the jewel.

The Gothic style of Toledo cathedral is not as pure as that of other Spanish cathedrals, such as those at Burgos and Leon. It has more of a Spanish style, lacking something of their gracefulness. The first architect to work on the building was probably Martín, a Frenchman. He was followed by his countryman, Petrus Petri (Pedro, son of Pedro). It is for this reasons that the lines of the cathedral take those at Bourges and Le Mans as models.

Floor area: the cathedral itself covers 6,500 square metres. It is divided into the nave and four aisles, while the vaults of the aisles become less tall the further they are from the nave. Nevertheless, the last two aisles are wider, from left to right, an original feature of this church. If all the ancillary buildings and cloisters are included, the area covered by the cathedral is greater than 10,000 square metres.

Length: 120 metres, with a maximum width of 60 metres. The nave is 32 metres high, while this is successively reduced in the aisles, down to a height of 12 metres.

8 *Transept window*

Rose window

Its vaults are supported by a total of 88 columns, while there are 750 richly coloured windows in its walls. These were created and put into place by artists from all over Europe, including ones from Spain, France, Germany, Belgium and the Netherlands. The creation of the windows took some 150 years, basically from the 14th to the 16th centuries.

Dating the windows would be quite easy, if one studied heraldry first, as normally the top of each window shows the shield of the archbishop who was governing the Diocese at the time it was made.

The main door is at the foot of the nave. This is always closed, due to a tradition that it is only to be opened for Heads of State, crown princes, Monarchs, and Presidents on official visits. Even archbishops only pass through this door on the day on which they take position of the See.

In this century, as well as for the Monarchs of Spain, the door has been opened for the Prince and Princess of Wales, the Prince and Princess of Japan (who are now Emperors), and the Monarchs of Italy, Jordan, the Netherlands and Belgium. It was also opened for the Presidents of the Philippines, Argentina, France and Portugal, and the only Pope to have visited the cathedral to date, John Paul II, in 1982.

In the front wall, which we can see in the background, forming the Choir, there are three open spaces occupied by small chapels. The one on the left, known as the Chapel of Christ Lying Down, has long been the object of especial veneration by the people of Toledo. Within it the magnificent carving by the Dutch artist, Copin, is on view.

The small chapel in the middle is that of the Virgin of the Star. She is of old the patron saint of wool dealers. At her feet is the tomb of the simple and holy archbishop of Toledo, Valero y Losa. He was from the Province of Cuenca (the town of Villanueva de la Jara), and was not raised to the rank of cardinal because of his short term of office.

On the right is the chapel of Saint Catalina. It contains the figures of her and two other saints, those of St Luke with the bull, and St Lucia with her eyes on a small plate. There were produced by the workshop of Copin, the master craftsman.

Although the Choir does interrupt the view, this inconvenience is made up for by the amazing decoration of its three walls and exterior. These show a series of biblical scenes step by step, by unknown artists of the 14th century. The narrate the first two books of the bible, Genesis and Exodus, in a simple folk idiom. This is the «Biblia Pauperorum» the bible of the poor, by which any child or adult unable to read could, with spoken aid, come to learn the Holy Book. Knowledge of the bible was thereby passed down from one generation to the next. This is a material representation in an almost childlike manner of the bible, only lacking balloons coming from the characters' mouths to give it the form of a comic. But given the high degree of illiteracy current at the time of their creation, they had to be explained by the spoken word instead.

But there is yet more. If we stand looking at the Choir from behind it, then the wall on the right shows several scenes that do not figure in the bible, and which are therefore apocryphal. There are five successive scenes, after the one next to the corner, which show one of the five extant versions of the death of Adam.

This is unique in Europe, and the only other comparable work is in the church of a small town in Germany. This curious scene is worth close attention. Adam is tired of life, for the bible (Genesis V, 5) states that he lived for 930 years. If the years then were as long as they are now, his tiredness is understandable. But he is not only exhausted due to the weight of years, but also because he has been working hard, cutting down trees. This is shown by the ground in the scenes, which is covered in branches and leaves. One tree is still standing. When his work is finished, Adam brings his hands together and asks God for death.

The third scene shows Adam with Eve. She is wearing Moorish dress, lacking only a veil over her face. They are calling their son, Seth, to send him to heaven to collect the oil of mercy which God had promised them, when he expelled them from Eden for having eaten the forbidden fruit.

The fourth scene shows Seth arriving at the gates of heaven. When asked by the Angel on the gate, St Michael, why he is there, Seth states his purpose. As Michael is unaware of the existence of the oil, he allows Seth to look over the gate (which, given the time this was made, is Gothic). Seth sees a tree that has been stripped of its bark. Its roots are buried in the jaws of a monstrous animal, where the head of a man emerges. At the top of the tree is the small figure of a crying baby. Once Seth has seen this, the angel gives him three seeds from the tree, to be placed in Adam's mouth when he dies.

The next scene shows the burial of Adam, with the chorus of professional mourners. We suppose that Seth does as the angel told him, for in the last scene a tree has sprouted from Adam's tomb. From a single trunk three separate branches emerge, each carved with great precision. One is a cedar branch, another is cypress and the third is pine. These branches symbolize the three distinct personages emerging from a single God: the Father, the Son, and the Holy Spirit.

This curious legend finishes here, and the scenes go back to showing standard biblical events. The first of these is of Noah's ark floating on the waters, which are now almost calm. A dove is shown on the roof of the ark, with the olive branch in its beak. The next scene shows the ark with the sons of Noah (Ham, Shem and Japheth) under it. Their father is lying on the ground, drunk. Helped by his brothers, Ham covers the nudity of his father. They cover their faces with their hands so as not to look upon him (Genesis IX, 23).

On the wall opposite the last of these biblical scenes is an enormous painting of Saint Christopher (the Carrier of Christ). This follows Western ichonographic techniques, showing the Saint as the aid to pilgrims. He is shown as a giant, with a crook of palm wood.

The popularity of this saint grew when the popular belief spread that those who had looked at a figure of Saint Christopher were freed from the possibility of sudden death. Large figures of the Saint were painted, so that even those in the worst possible personal or physical situations, or under the most unfavourable conditions, would be able to see the gigantic figure.

Nowadays Saint Christopher is considered to be the patron saint of drivers. This is a continuation of his traditional role as a helper of pilgrims and travellers, protecting against the risk of sudden death.

The fresco painting was repainted or repaired by Gabriel de la Rueda in 1638, and has recently been restored.

We now arrive at the transept. This is impressive as a whole, and is absolutely full of art treasures.

THE CHOIR

The elegant railings around the Choir are by Domingo de Céspedes, and were finished in 1548.

Prayer took place here at the Canonical Hours, at least in contemporary times, twice a day, in the morning and evening.

The Choir as a whole is the most important set of Renaissance sculpture in Spain, without forgetting its base, which was made during the end of the Gothic period.

Once again, this is the work of several European artists. Alonso de Berruguete, from Paredes de Nava, Palencia, is the Spanish representative here. He is known as the Spanish Michael Angelo, and created all the stalls along the upper left wall, looking from the entrance to the Choir. Felipe de Borgoña, who was French, carved the stalls on the upper right. There are 35 seats on each side in the upper level.

Both artists carved in walnut wood, showing saints, patriarchs and prophets, crowning their achievement with a superb alabaster frieze. This shows a multitude of biblical characters, all of whom are identified by name, inscribed at the foot of each figure.

Detail of the choir: the siege of Granada

The 35 seats in the lower stalls were the work of «Rodericus Germanicus» (Rodrigo the German). This is truly a work of its times, as it virtually amounts to news reporting, substituting a gouge and walnut wood for pen and paper. In chronological order the artist depicts the last ten years of the long war of reconquest, started almost eight hundred years earlier by Pelayo, in the mountains of Asturias. The final ten years of the war are shown to begin with the reconquest of Alhama, Granada, and they end with the taking of the capital of the last Arab kingdom left on the Iberian Peninsular, Granada, on January 2nd, 1492. This date corresponds with the backs of the final two seats on the left and right of the access stairs to the archbishop's seat. But before them, on the lower stalls of both sides of the Choir, the day to day and year to year story is told of many towns. These include some in the Province of Malaga (Marbella, Comares, Velez Málaga and Ronda), Granada (Salobreña, Almuñecar, Loja, Guadix), Almeria (Mojacar, Nijar, Velez Blanco and Velez Rubio), amongst others. Their names are carved into the wood, while most of the towns themselves are easily recognizable.

These scenes form a valuable historical document, showing details not only of clothing, but also the riding gear, swords and artillery used, etc.

Detail of the lower choir: the taking of Gor (Granada)

At each seat there is a misericord (mercy seat), a piece of projecting wood that allowed older clerics to rest when they had to stand for long periods.

On the upper part of the railings there are the words «Psalle, Psille» (sing and be quiet). This was placed there as a warning to any Choir member who may have been tempted to start talking to the man next to him.

Berruguete crowned this magnificent work with a sculpted group of figures in alabaster, above the archbishop's chair. This shows the transfiguration of Christ, on Mount Tabor in Israel, accompanied by the prophets Elijah and Moses.

The choir: the transfiguration of Christ 17

The Great Lectern

The choir: the transfiguration of Christ

The furnishings of the Choir are completed by two great organs. One, known as «the old organ» is baroque, and dates from the 18th century (1758). The other is neoclassical, from the end of the same century (1798) and is known as «the new organ».

There is a statue and standard on the pillar next to the baroque organ. This statue is of Diego Lopez de Haro, a lord from the Basque country, in remembrance of his help at the Battle of las Navas de Tolosa (1212). He was also a great benefactor to the cathedral.

One cannot leave the Choir without looking at the White Virgin. This magnificent sculpture of the French school is in a single piece of white marble, from which its name is taken. Her smile is maternal, enigmatic and tender, and is returned in kind by her Son.

The king of Spain has a seat in this Choir, as an Honorary Canon.

18th c. neoclassic organ

18th c. baroque organ

The lectern: detail

20 *The White Virgin*

THE CHANCEL

On leaving the Choir we are confronted by the Chancel. This is enclosed by one of the masterworks of Spanish grille making. It is the work of Francisco de Villalpando, and, given the date on which it was finished (1548) it is surmounted by the imperial shield of the Hapsburg dynasty, to which the king reigning then, Carlos V, belonged. The author signed his work very modestly, on the left hand corner, with the short latin legend «Labor ubicumque» - «Work everywhere».

The Transept

22 *High Chapel: triforium*

High altar piece

The Early 20th Century French writer, Maurice Barres, described this chancel as the most luxuriously furnished room in the world. He was thinking above all of the gigantic altar piece, a symbol of European art. 27 artists from France, Germany, Belgium, the Netherlands and Spain worked on this from 1498 to 1504. Some carved, others coloured or made the figures. They created one of the last marvels of Gothic art, now restricted to wood by the

High altar piece: the Nativity by Copin

new style coming from Italy. A notable feature of this altar piece is the way it maintains a uniform perspective all the way up to the top. This is achieved by the use of diminutive figures at the bottom, and steadily larger ones as rows become higher. For the Calvary scene at the top, the figures used are about 3 metres high.

On each side of the altar piece there are the royal tombs of monarchs of the kingdoms of Castile and Castile - Leon. On the right in the foreground is the tomb of king Sancho IV. He was the son of king Alfonso X and queen Violante, Princess of Aragón, the daughter of king Jaime I. The other tomb here is that of Pedro, who was Lord of Aguilar de Campóo, Liébana and Pernia. He was the bastard son of Alfonso XI and Lady Leonor de Guzmán. On the left at the bottom is the tomb of the titular Emperor Alfonso VII, son of queen Urraca and Raimundo de Borgoña, and who founded the Burgundian dynasty. He was married to Lady Berenguela, the daughter of Ramón Berenguer IV, the Count of Barcelona, and their son was Sancho III, king only of Castile, who is buried at his side.

High altar piece: detail

25

The tomb of the famous archbishop of Toledo, cardinal Mendoza, occupies the left wall. He was known in his time as «The Third king of Spain». He placed his cross on the Watchtower of the Alhambra in Granada, on the day the city surrendered and the monarchs entered it. He was of an aristocratic Castilian family, and was born in Guadalajara. His father was the celebrated Marquis de Santillana, author of the famous «Serranilla» poems. This tomb is one of the first Renaissance works in Spain, and is attributed to the school of one of two Italian artists, Andrea Sansovino or Domenico Fanceilli.

At the top of the stairs here there is a group of seven pieces, six candelabra and a cross. They were made of gold plated bronze in London, in 1790.

Before leaving this chapel, one should notice the two pillars on left and right, near the royal tombs. On top of the pillar on the left, accompanied by the statues of several kings and next to the tomb of cardinal Mendoza, a strange bearded figure can be seen holding a sort of crook. This pillar is known as «The Shepherd's pillar» because of this. According to a folk tradition, the victory of king Alfonso VIII over the Almohad faction at the battle of Navas de Tolosa (1212) was gained thanks to a shepherd called Martín Alhaja. He showed the Castilian army the path they could use to take their enemy by surprise. As he indicated the way they were to go by placing a cow's skull there, the grateful king gave him the surname of «Cow's Head» (Cabeza de Vaca).

On the opposite pillar, on the right, a figure of a man dressed in course woollen cloth stands out amongst a group of archbishops. The Christian version of the tradition about this figure, which does not entirely agree with the Arab version, says that it represents the Chief of the Arab community (Alfaquí) in Toledo. The archbishop and the queen broke the agreement that Alfonso VI had made with the Arab community, to respect the Main Mosque and allow it to continue as an Islamic place of worship. They consecrated it as a Christian church, and the king rushed back to Toledo so that justice could be done. The Alfaquí, Abu Walid, went out of the city with a group of nobles to meet the king, so that he would pardon those who had broken the agreement, which he did in fact do.

To honour such a tolerant gesture, a statue of the man who made it was placed on this pillar. This is a highly unusual honour, in giving a man who was not a Christian a monument in such an important place, within the chancel of the cathedral itself.

The Great Lamp hangs at the centre of the transept. It belonged to the national Congress House, and was presented to the cathedral by the government in 1863. It used only to be lit for matins on Easter Wednesday.

The right interior facade of the transept should not be missed. This is crowned by a magnificent organ, known as «The Emperor's», which is the oldest of all those within the cathedral. It dates from the mid 16th century, and its case is made entirely of stone. It is traditionally played on the day of Corpus Christi, when the procession returns to the cathedral, which is one of the most impressive moments of the ceremony. Nevertheless, it is also played in concerts, and at some important functions and ceremonies. Under the organ the facade is lavishly decorated, with the Coronation of the Virgin Mary and the Tree of Jesse as central themes. The Tree of Jesse is above another door into the cathedral, known as the Door of the Lions because of the lions sculpted in marble on the outside.

Detail of the Emperor´s Door

28 *The Emperor's Organ*

There are two tombs at the bottom of this wall. The one on the left is that of a canon, a member of the cathedral chapter. The tomb on the right holds the ashes of the archbishop from Navarre, the Dominican friar Bartolomé de Carranza. They were brought to Toledo from Rome on December 10th, 1993, on the express wishes of the archbishop of Toledo, cardinal Marcelo González Martín. Archbishop Bartolomé was a victim of the Inquisition after holding office for only nine months. He was maliciously detained by the tribunal of the Inquisition, and was imprisoned and tried for seventeen years, until the Pope ordered his release. He died in Toledo a few days after being released, in 1576.

On entering the triforium, at a part of the church which is commonly known as the «Girola» because it is here that the building «turns» into the apse, a gallery of many curved arches can be seen. This is an important Mudejar note in an otherwise Gothic building with some Renaissance structures and decorations.

It is as one moves towards the apse that something really unexpected and spectacular comes into view.

THE TRANSPARENTE

A masterwork of the Spanish baroque, this is praised by some and hated by others. Nevertheless, it is now coming to gain a more balanced critical appraisal. It was constructed from 1721 to 1732.

Although it is the work of a team of craftsmen, only one, Narciso, the Head of Works of the cathedral, signed it.

It was the creation of the Tomé family (the father and three sons) who came from the city of Toro, in the province of Zamorra. In the absence of the father, his sons carried on with the project. They were helped by a man from the same part of the country as they themselves, the worker canon Fernando Merino. They combined three art forms: architecture, painting and sculpture. To these they added a fourth and natural agency: light. An almost magical effect was thereby created by the entire work.

Marble from Carrara (Italy) and Urda, Castañar and Montesclaros (Toledo) was used, together with alabaster from Honrubia (province of Cuenca), jasper from Socuellamos (province of Ciudad Real) and Saelices (Cuenca), together with stuccoes and countless bronze ornaments.

30 *The «Transparente»*

The great altar piece: the «Transparente»

Narciso was born in 1694, and was the middle son of three brothers. He was a self-taught architect, and at the age of 27 produced his most daring work: he broke through the vault at the key point of the church, breaking its balance, and running the risk of causing a general fall of the roof.

Diego was the youngest of the three brothers, and was born in 1696. He specialized in sculpting and engraving, and made many of the figures here, in Italian marble from Carrara.

The first-born son, Andrés (1688) was a painter and sculptor. He painted all the areas around the sculptures and the enormous opening of the Transparente (which had been made by his brothers) al fresco, with scenes «genesis» from the Apocalypse and the Book of Judges. The brothers worked with a team of gilders and bronzesmiths.

There is a great altar piece in front of this, which occupies the whole rear wall of the chancel. Everything here centres on the Eucharist, showing biblical scenes. In the middle there is a hole that serves as a window into the area where the Holy Sacrament used to be kept. This window is surrounded by the four archangels, St Raphael, with the fish, St Michael, with his shield, St Gabriel with the bunch of lilies, and St Uriel, who is spreading incense. The Last Supper is shown above them, in alabaster.

On both sides of the niche which holds a statue of the Virgin, in the part nearest the floor, two scenes from the Book of Kings are shown. On the right, Abigail is shown kneeling before king David. On the left, king David is shown receiving the sword of Goliath from Ahimelech.

The cardinal archbishop who ordered this work is buried at the foot of the altar, which is a notable piece of inlaid marble. He was cardinal Astorga, from Gibraltar.

Next to this tomb there is another, which has its corresponding cardinal's hat hanging from the vault. This is the tomb of archbishop cardinal Moreno, the first person from America to attain this rank. He was born in Central America, in Guatemala, and was related to García Moreno, who was president of Ecuador.

Going back on our footsteps, we find the

The hollow of the «Transparente»

Detail of one of the bronzes (Narciso Tomé)

«Transparente»: Virgin with Child (Narciso Tomé)

CHAPTER HOUSE

This has two rooms, the anteroom and Hall. cardinal Cisneros ordered it to be built, in the early years of the 16th century.

The anteroom is a curious mixture of Renaissance and Arab influence, with magnificent panelling. It is decorated with paintings, friezes and furniture in Renaissance style. The cabinet on the right is an original, and dates from the 16th century, while the one on the left is a good 18th century copy.

A finely worked grille hanging on the right of the entrance contains a letter from king Alfonso XIII to the Chapter.

The Hall has a richly decorated coffered ceiling, in gilded wood. Once again, Arab and Renaissance styles alternate here. The frescos showing the life of Christ were all painted by Juan de Borgoña. He also painted the

The Chapter House Door

upper row of portraits of the Prelates of the See of Toledo. All of these are imaginary, except for the two last ones to the left of the archbishop's chair, which may be considered genuine as they are contemporary with the painter. These are the portraits of cardinals Mendoza and Cisneros.

The lower file of paintings does consist of real portraits, of which the first is that of cardinal Croy. The final portrait in this row is of the last archbishop before the current one, cardinal Enrique y Tarrancón, who died in 1994.

This collection of portraits expresses the greatness of the «Primal See of All Spain», through its archbishops, all of whom except three were cardinals, from the end of the 15th century to the present day. That these three were not made cardinals was due to the short time they held the office. They were archbishops Carranza, Valero y Losa, and García de Loaysa. As well as being prelates, most of the archbishops were also great patrons and guardians of art. Many of them also occupied important political positions. They came from Asturias, Catalonia and Andalusia, Extremadura and Valencia, Galicia and Navarre, Castilla - la - Mancha and Leon. Some were foreign, from France or Flanders. That they have continued in an uninterrupted line down to our own days enriches this diocese, making it universal and not at all provincial.

On the way from the Chapter House to the Sacristy, the largest two of the 31 chapels that make up the cathedral can be seen.

Craftwork in the Chapter House

THE CHAPEL OF SAINT ILDEFONSO

This is where the Albornoz family is buried. In the centre is the tomb of its founder, Gil Alvarez de Albornoz. He was from Cuenca, and was considered to be the greatest political genius of the Iberian peninsula. He was exiled in Castile because of his criticism of king Pedro I, before leaving for the Papal Court in Avignon. He was commissioned there to bring together the Papal States, which were disintegrating.

After working hard on recovering fortified towns in Papal lands, he died in Viterbo, near Rome. His remains were brought back to Toledo cathedral, as he had wished. The journey took almost a year. He was the founder of the famous College of Saint Clement, in Bologna, which is still functioning.

The chapel is dominated by a neoclassical marble altar piece. It is the work of Ventura Rodríguez, and shows the oft - repeated subject of the gift of the robe to Saint Ildefonso.

The tomb of Cardinal Gil de Albornoz

St. James´s Chapel

Luna Chapel: tomb of Juan de Cerezuela

The next large chapel is that dedicated to the Head of the Constabulary, and is similar to the one in Burgos cathedral.

The Luna family are buried here and in the crypt of the chapel. It is still used for the burial of the current owners, the Dukes of Infantado. In the centre are the tombs of the favourite of Don Juan II of Castile and Leon, Don Alvaro de Luna, and his wife, Doña Juana de Pimentel. D. Alvaro was executed in Valladolid by order of the king.

The chapel is presided over by an excellent altar piece showing the figure of Saint James as a pilgrim. There are portraits at the bottom by Sancho de Zamora of the donors.

Ceiling fresco in the Sacristy

Ceiling fresco in the Sacristy

39

THE SACRISTY

This is the climax of our visit to Toledo cathedral. It can be considered to be a true art gallery, set off by the fresco that covers its entire ceiling. This is the work of the Italian, Luca Giordano. He was also know as «Luca fa presto» («Fast Luke») due to the speed at which he apparently worked. People said that he was able to work at such speed because he held a brush in each hand, working with both at the same time.

The entire scene is dominated by the name of God in Hebrew, inscribed in the centre of the ceiling.

Fresco (detail)

The collection of paintings is incredible. There are 18 works by El Greco, together with others by Zurbarán, Bellini, Rafael, Rubens, Velázquez, etc. Here we will pay special attention to three works.

The Tears of St. Peter (El Greco)

The great work which presides over the room is by El Greco:

THE SPOLIATION

Together with his masterpiece in the church of Santo Tomé, «The Burial of the Count of Orgaz», this is one of El Greco's crowning achievements. Like the «Burial», this painting is also displayed in the place it was painted for, by special order of the cathedral.

When the cathedral Chapter ordered this painting, El Greco was still working on decorating the Cistercian monastery church of Santo Domingo with altar pieces and paintings.

He was free to choose his subject. The easiest option would have been for him to paint a Crucifixion, of the type that may be seen in many church sacristies, usually hanging together with a mirror.

However, he chose a scene that went perfectly with the use to which the room was put, as it was where those who officiated changed into their liturgical robes. The painting shows Christ being robbed of his clothes before making the supreme sacrifice.

Greco uses a surprising technique to concentrate our attention on the figure of Christ: colour. The colour used makes the figure of Christ stand out from the whole crowd around him.

If it were not for this exultant colour, the tremendous anachronism to the left of Christ would be noticed by more visitors. This is a Roman soldier, dressed in beautiful 16th century armour. The signature of the painter is on a paper in the bottom right hand corner. As always, he signed in Greek, his native language.

On the right, under the arch which contains an altar table, there is another painting, one equally modern and up - to - date as Greco's.

The Spoliation. El Greco

THE KISS OF JUDAS, by GOYA

This sublime painter from Aragón was the precursor of all modern Spanish art. He shows Jesus as the central figure, with Judas Iscariot approaching to kiss him on the cheek. Here too, Jesus is surrounded by a crowd, and to make his figure stand out Goya makes subtle use of light. The source of this light is not visible, only its reflection from the figure on the left of Christ. This illuminates Jesus, and in combination with the yellowish white of his clothing, makes him stand out from the crowd.

Although both El Greco's and Goya's paintings show the figure of Christ, they express two different theological viewpoints, according to the different scenes shown, both of which formed part of a single story.

Saint John's gospel gives us the Eastern version of events. This evangelist believed that the maximum humiliation of Christ was to be God made man, after which he triumphed on the cross. Greco therefore paints the spoliation of Christ with a purple tunic, symbol of royalty and following the description of the evangelist. Raising his eyes to heaven, Christ has already accepted the death which is to glorify him.

On the other hand, Goya expresses Western traditions started in the letters of Saint Paul. In this painting of the «Kiss of Judas», Christ is humiliated not only by being made man, but also because he has to accept the cross as a condemned man, «just one of so many». This picture shows Christ totally humbled and resigned. His eyes look down at the ground, and he wears a white tunic, symbol of mockery and derision.

The Kiss of Judas: Goya

At the exit of the sacristy, on the left and next to the door, the third great painting of the three here may be seen. This is the painting of Pope Paul III, by Titian. The play of light it shows over the red velvet, the aged hands and the technique used to paint the hairs of the beard, all go towards making this one of the finest Renaissance portraits in Europe.

Paul III

Once these three paintings have been admired, a walk can be taken around the room. After the Papal portrait by Titian, there is the Virgin of the Veil, by the Italian, Raphael. The first arch contains one of the finest works of primitive European art. This panel painting shows the burial of Christ, and is signed by Giovanni Bellini, who was Venetian. Above the painting there is an Ecce Homo, with donor.

Over each of the pilasters around the sacristy there is a one of an important collection of works by El Greco. This is composed of 13 paintings, of the 12 apostles and Christ. This is without doubt the finest of the known collections of these pictures. They were copied by the painter in his studio, and this is the first of the series painted between 1605 - 1610.

The figures of St John the Evangelist, St Matthew, St Paul and St Luke stand out. St Luke was not actually one of the apostles, although he is shown here as such. He substitutes St Simon, and shows us a picture of the Virgin in an open book. Nor is St Matthias shown, as he is replaced by St Paul.

The first display cabinet on the right holds a surprising carving in wood, of St Francis of Assisi in ecstasy. This is by the gifted pupil of Alonso Cano, Pedro de Mena, who was from Granada. It is one of his masterworks.

St. Luke

50 *St. Francis of Assisi: by Pedro de Mena*

In the lower part of a small arch lined with velvet are the remains of the 7th century Visigoth kings, Wamba and Recesvinto, as the inscription on its top explains. These remains were brought to the cathedral solemnly and publicly in 1845.

St. Joseph and child Jesus

The next arch along contains El Greco's splendid sketch showing St. Joseph and the Child Jesus. This was the prelude to his great work, that is still in its place of origin: St Joseph's Chapel, in Toledo. It is one of the few examples in the history of art in which St Joseph is shown as a young man. He has his powerful arm resting on the shoulders of the Child, who in turn seeks paternal protection. This shows us the tender communication between father and child.

El Greco signs on his usual piece of white paper, and there is a small landscape of Toledo at the foot of the painting. This shows two features often included by El Greco in his paintings: San Servando Castle and Alcántara bridge (the Arab name of which means simply «the bridge»). On the right are two buildings which are emblematic of the city: the Alcázar and the cathedral.

There is a small picture on each side of this sketch. They are painted on wooden panels, and show Young Jesus and the Virgin Mary. They were painted by Antonio Raphael Mengs, a German painter from Aussig (Bohemia). He had been called to Spain by king Carlos III, and was an academic painter, with a smooth style.

Young Jesus (Antonio Rafael Mengs)

Above the work by Greco there is a painting of St Ines, by Van Dyck.

A door opens into the room known as the Vestry. Here the magnificent collection of paintings is continued, presided over by a large walnut cabinet and an ivory crucifix that was presented by cardinal Portocarro. There is also a painting on a wooden panel by Luca Giordano, showing the Baptism of Christ. The collection in this room is completed by works of Van Dyck, Velázquez, Ribera, Rubens, Guido Reni, the Bassano brothers and «Mario dei Fiori» (Mario of the Flowers) who specialized in floral themes. The ceiling was painted by Claudio Coello, who was from Madrid, and José Ximenez.

Another room contains two symbolic Moroccan standards. These belonged to the Benimerin or Merinid dynasty, and were captured by king Alfonso XI at the Battle of Salado (1340) which was fought against the army of Emperor Abul Hassan.

The next room contains a large collection of ecclesiastical ornaments and embroideries from the 15th to the 19th centuries.

On returning to the sacristy, in the next arch a painting by the Murcian painter Pedro de Orrente can be seen, showing the apparition of the Toledan saint, Leocardia, to archbishop St Idelfonso and king Recesvinto. This may be his masterpiece, and mixes Venetian influences with those of the school of El Greco.

St. Francis (El Greco)

The last picture, over the pilaster on the right, is known as the «Dolorosa». It was painted by Luis de Morales, a 16th century painter known as «The Divine». He was from Extremadura, but lived in Toledo. Its colours are delicate and luminous, and the painting is highly mystical. It was inexpertly enlarged to make it fit the same size of frame as El Greco's apostles. The painting following the one by Goya is a magnificent Holy Family by Van Dyck, one of the finest artists of the Flemish school.

The glass showcase in front of and to the right of the Spoliation contains two reliquaries, together with a stone lithographic

The Holy Family (Van Dyck)

plaque from the low middle ages. This shows the cycle of 12 Holy Days, from the Annunciation to the death of the Virgin. The «deesis» (the intercession of Mary and St John before Christ as judge) is shown in the upper part.

An outstanding piece is the silver urn that contains the remains of St Eugene, archbishop of Toledo. It was made in the 12th century, and also holds the arm donated by Luis VII of France.

The lower part shows some objects found in 1947, when royal sarcophagi in the chancel were opened.

The gothic sword belonged to Don Fernando de Antequera, king of Aragón, following the Compromise of Caspe.

La Dolorosa

On the other side of the altar, together with the Spoliation, there are two reliquaries from Limoge. They date from the end of the 12th century.

There is a seated Virgin with Child. This is silver plated, and may date from the 12th century. It is known as St Mary of Toledo. A bishop's crook from the same era is displayed beneath the seated Virgin. It was found in excavations undertaken around Toledo in the 18th century.

Together with several other reliquaries, the next showcase contains one in the form of the Virgin. It is made of ivory, and dates from the 13th or 14th century. French - Gothic in style, it shows the typical curve of an elephant's tusk.

Below this is an enormous chalice, with its paten. It is known in Toledo as the chalice of the Moorish Queen, and could be one of those left to the cathedral by king Alfonso VIII.

The following arch contains a picture showing the prayer in the garden. It is the work of José Ramos, of the 18th century.

The next work is the great painting by Luis Tristán, «Christ on the Cross».

The next arch contains a tryptic by Juan de Borgoña, as well as a portrait of the donor, and El Greco's painting of Christ on the Cross. It is the property of the College of Noble Ladies, Toledo.

The fourth and last showcase contains one of the jewels of Portuguese precious metal craftsmanship. This is the great gold - plated silver processional cross which heads the procession at Corpus Christi every year. It was donated to archbishop Carrillo de Acuña in the 15th century by the king of Portugal, Alfonso V. In style, it belongs to the same family as the great crosses at Alcobaça, Guimaraes and Coimbra.

The crown is a modern work, and was made at the Granda workshops in Madrid, in 1926. Financed by popular subscription, it was used for the canonical crowning of the patron saint of Toledo. It is made of precious metals and stones, and weighs almost 12 kilogrammes.

The figurine in gold, emerald and precious stones is of St Anne and the Virgin.

The last arch holds the tomb of cardinal Borbón. He was grandson, nephew, uncle and cousin of four kings of Spain. He was president of the Defence Junta that was set up to fight the invasion by Napoleon. He was the main patron supplying the ornaments and decoration of the sacristy.

The series of pictures terminates with a good painting by Crespi, who was Italian. It shows Jesus and the Samaritan woman, as well as a portrait of a cardinal by Zurbarán.

The other walls of this great hall are covered by many tapestries, the work of Luca Giordano and other artists.

Jesus and the Samaritan Woman

On leaving the sacristy, next to it, we come to the

SANCTUARY CHAPEL

This is formed by an ante-chapel and chapel. They were finished in 1616, and were the work of the architects Vergara the Younger and Monegro.

It is here that the patron saint of the city is kept. Known as the «Virgin of the Sagrario» (sanctuary) this is an interesting sitting figure, made of medlar wood and covered in silver. It dates either from the end of the 12th century or the early years of the 13th.

The chapel is completely lined in different sorts of marble, with paintings by Carduccio and Caxés.

Sanctuary Virgin

The 18th century Italian precious metal smith Fanelli designed the throne on which the image sits. It is made of gold plated silver, and took 17 years to complete.

The statue is dressed for certain yearly festivals, following a centuries - old tradition.

More archbishops of Toledo are interred here than in any other single place. A total of nine have their tombs here, four in the same chapel. The Catalonians Gomá (1940) and Plá y Deniel (1968) are inhumed at the end of the chapel, on the left and right, respectively. The Valencian, Reig, is entombed in the centre of the chapel (1927). He was unique as a cardinal, in that he lived through the three states of bachelor, married man and widow. The remains of the founder of the chapel, Sandoval (1618) who was from Burgos, are in the funeral urn under the arch on the left. The magnificent lamp of rock crystal and bronze was made in Vienna in the 18th century, and was presented by the Duke of Infantado.

The ante-chapel contains the following tombs: that of the Franciscan cardinal Alameda (1872) was from Madrid, and is known to history as Father Cirilio. Following this is the tomb of Monescillo, a Franciscan from La Mancha (1897). The tomb of Portocarrero (1709) is outside this chapel, with its famous epigraph of «Here lies dust, ashes and nothing». The last tombs are those of another Franciscan, from Asturias, cardinal Aguirre (1914) and Paya (1885) who was from Alicante.

THE CLOCK DOOR (interior)

The other door in the transept is known as the Clock Door. This name comes from the clock placed above it in 1545. This has only one hand, and shows the canonical hours, at which all the clerics in the cathedral went to pray. For the rest of the town, the chiming of the hours, half hours and quarter hours was appreciated, as it gave a more exact idea of the time than was otherwise available in those days. Above the clock face, two figures used to simulate striking the bell at the appropriate times.

Immediately after this door is the great Chapel of St Peter. This used to be the parish chapel of the cathedral. It contains several tombs, amongst which is that of one of the more recent archbishops, cardinal Inguanzo. He was from Asturias, and died in 1836. The tomb of cardinal Sancha is in front of this chapel. It is always covered in flowers, and he is undergoing the process of beatification. He came from Burgos, and died in 1909.

A little further on, in front of the Chapel of St Teresa, is the tomb of cardinal Almaraz from Salamanca (1922) with its corresponding cardinal's hat.

60 *The Chapel of St. Peter*

THE CHAPEL OF THE DESCENT

Before reaching the end of the nave, there is a small chapel on the left. It is crowned with a large gothic pinnacle, and marks a spot of great significance for the Toledan people. This is where tradition has it that the presbytery of the old church of St Mary stood. It was here that the Virgin descended in the 7th century, to invest archbishop St Ildefonso, as is shown by the alabaster altar piece. On the right of the altar, protected by a small grille, is the stone on which the virgin placed her foot when she descended.

The representation of this event virtually became the emblem of the cathedral. It can be seen in many places, both inside and outside the building.

This chapel is also the spot where cardinal Moscoso, from Galicia (1665) is buried. He was of the noble house of Denia, and his image can be seen on the front of the altar. His cardinal's hat hangs from the ceiling.

The Chapel of the Descent: central altar

62 *Treasury Door*

THE TREASURY

Just by the door where we came in, and through which we will shortly leave the cathedral, is the Chapel of the Tower. It is known by this name as it is in the base of the tower itself. It is also known as the Chapel of St John the Baptist, and it was here that a century ago the most noteworthy pieces of the cathedral treasure were placed on view. The monstrance is the most outstanding item, and it is used every year in the procession of Corpus Christi, which has been declared of International Interest for Tourism. This procession covers about 2 kilometres through the intricate streets of the city.

Detail of the centre: the monstrance

The great writer Galdós described the monstrance in two words: «Colossal jewel».

Basically, it is divided into two parts: the central piece is a small monstrance in pure gold, made in Barcelona at the end of the 15th century by the Catalan artist Jaume Aimerich (Jaime Alberique) for the personal use of Catholic queen Isabel I. When the queen died, some of her personal belongings were sold to pay for several stipulations of her will. The canons bidded for it in the auction of the queen's goods, which was held in Toro in 1505.

During the first third of the 16th century, the cathedral Chapter decided that they wished for a canopy to hold their beautiful gold monstrance, which was of such historical significance. The German silversmith Heinrich Erfert (Enrique Arfe) was asked to make this new silver piece, which was gold plated at a later date.

The pedestal was added in the mid 18th century. It is composed of four angels holding the platform for the two above - mentioned pieces.

St. Luis´s bible

It was made in Toledo, following the plans of the creator of the transparente, Narciso Tomé. The total weight of all three parts is approximately 200 kilogrammes.

Amongst the countless and valuable objects which the treasury contains is the so - called Bible of St Luis. This is on the right, and is a magnificent French manuscript from the 13th century. Its text is in French and Latin, and it is illustrated with miniatures. This is an «annotated» bible, in that it connects scenes from the Old and New Testaments.

The great imperial crown of the patron saint of the city is also outstanding. It dates from the mid 17th century, and is the work of the Toledan goldsmith Francisco Andres Salinas.

The cross painted on wood is also notable. It is by the Italian Fray Angelico de Fiésole. On one side Christ is shown still alive, while on the back he is shown dead, with his head bowed down onto his chest. This was presented to the cathedral after the Spanish civil war (1936 - 1939) by the then head of the Italian government.

A superb coffered ceiling in plaster which recalls some of those in the Alhambra at Granada covers this chapel under the great tower.

66 *The Croos of Friar Angelico*

On the way out, our visit is completed by contemplation of the main facade, which dates from the 15th century. It was renovated and reinforced with buttresses in the 18th century. The dome covering the never completed second tower is the work of El Greco's son, Jorge Manuel Theotocopoulos. It dates from 1622.

The doors in the centre are covered in bronze, showing the shields of Castile and Leon. They are dated 1377.

The great tower on the left of the facade is ninety one and a half metres high. The three sections into which it is divided can be seen clearly. The first holds the chapel which now contains the cathedral treasury.

The second section used to contain the living quarters of the bell ringer or doorkeeper.

The third section, or strong room, was used as an ecclesiastical prison. Above it is the belfry, which still holds nine bells. The largest of these is known as the «Gorda» («the big one»). This is one of the largest in the world, together with others in Russia and the United States. It weighs more than 17 tons, and was cast in the 18th century.

Above this belfry there are three more bells, together with a large rattle that used to be used in Easter Week.

A popular folk saying mentions the famous «big one»:

> Toledo for its bell,
> Leon for its church,
> Benavente for its clock
> And Villalón for its boundary column.

The doors on either side of the transept are also worth looking at from the outside.

On the left, and at the end of the street known as the Chapinería, or Feria, the Door of the Clock can be seen. The face on the outside corresponds to that which can be seen inside.

68 *«The Big One»: painted by Angel Lucio Ludeña*

Facade

70 *Main door*

Main door

This is the oldest of all the cathedral doors. It is covered in biblical images, together with a series of animals and other features. All are protected by a great pointed arch, which was constructed from the 13th to the 15th century.

Above the arch there is an 18th century decorative frame for the clock face. It is crowned by the image of a saint holding a cross in his hand.

Behind this, the great gothic window can be seen. This is the oldest of all those in the cathedral, and dates from the 14th century.

On the opposite side of the transept is the Door of the Lions. It takes its name from the marble lions on the columns which hold the railings.

This is a delicate gothic construction from the 15th century, by Egas, an artist from Brussels. This end of the right hand side of the transept is reinforced by buttresses, and was decorated in neoclassical style in the 18th century. This can be seen above the large pointed arch, which is similar to that over the Clock Door. 11 medallions in high relief show prophets and patriarchs around the Virgin Mary, who is shown on the central medallion. Above these, a large statue of St Augustine at prayer crowns the door.

72 *Clock door*

The Door of the Lions

74 *Door of the Lions: detail*

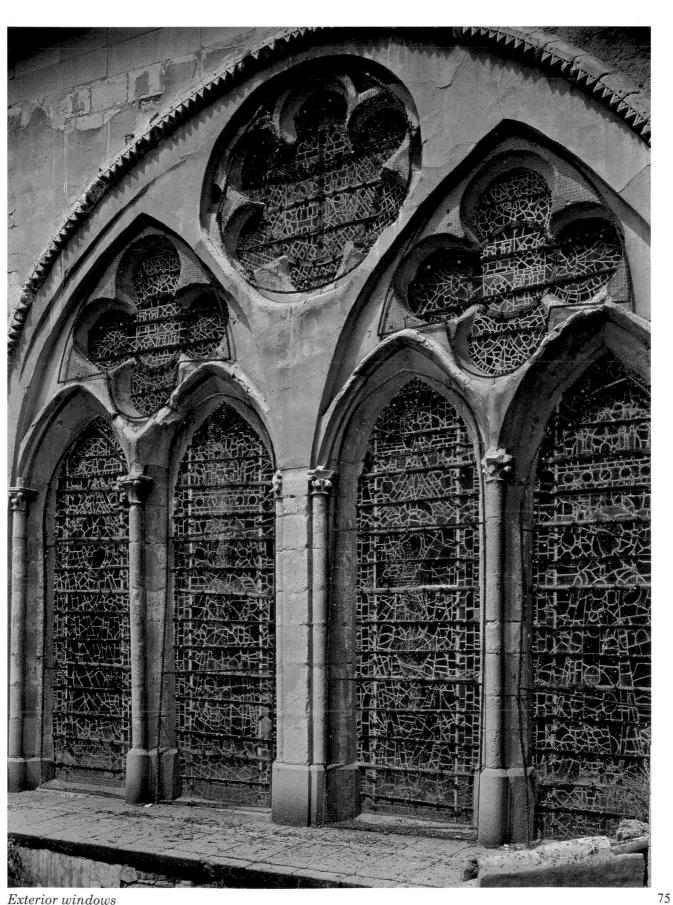

Exterior windows

76 *Buttresses and roofs: Cathedral*

78 *Mozarab chapel: detail*

APPENDIX

Other areas of the cathedral which are normally closed, or are more difficult to visit include:

THE MOZARAB CHAPEL

This occupies the base of what was to have been the second tower. It gets is name from the Mass said there every day. This famous rite is also known as the Isidorian, Gothic or Cisnerian mass. It is most widely known as the Mozarab mass, as it was kept on by the Catholic Christian communities which were tolerated during the Arab domination of Spain. It survived after the Christian reconquest, in spite of the imposition of the Latin rite.

During the early years of the 16th century, the great cardinal Cisneros reaffirmed the Mozarab rite. He founded and equipped this chapel, published new prayer books and created a special Chapter of clerics within the cathedral to maintain the rite. It is still fully alive today, following the most recent reform. Toledo also has two Mozarab churches, supported by the large community of 1,000 families who are the descendants of the early Christian community.

Outstanding features of this chapel include the friezes at the end and in the front of the entrance. They show the conquest of the city of Oran (Algeria) by cardinal Cisneros in 1509, and were painted by a French artist, Juan of Burgundy. A central altar piece presides over the chapel, with another two, one on each side. All of three of these came from the Transito Synagogue.

These works surround a beautiful mosaic, showing the Virgin. It was produced by the papal workshops in Rome at the end of the 18th century. Above this, there is a crucifix made of Mexican fennel root wood.

There is a small choir with stalls carved by Arnot, a German.

Mozarab chapel: craftwork

THE CHAPEL OF THE NEW KINGS

On the other side of the church (also known as the apse or «girola») there is another chapel which is not currently in use. Until modern times a Chapter called the «King's Chaplains» maintained the rite here, but they have now utterly disappeared.

This chapel was founded by Enrique II of Castile and Leon in 1374. However, it has only been in its present location since 1530. It was constructed by the architects Egas and Covarrubias.

The tomb of Juana Manuel

The altar pieces which decorate this chapel are from the 18th century. They are by Ventura Rodríguez, and contain paintings by Mariano Salvador Maella.

This chapel contains the tombs of virtually an entire dynasty of the kingdom of Castile and Leon, the Trastámara family. The only members of this dynasty not interred here are Isabel, the Catholic Queen, who is buried in Granada, her father, Juan II, who is buried in Burgos, and Enrique IV, whose tomb is at Guadalupe (Caceres).

On the right are the mausoleums of Enrique II and his queen, Doña Juana Manuel. On the left is the tomb of Enrique III, the first Prince of Asturias. It was he who brought the Canary Islands into the Kingdom of Castile and Leon. The tomb of his wife is also here. She was queen Catalina of Lancaster, granddaughter of Edward III of England.

In the presbytery and next to the main altar piece, the tomb of king Juan I is on the left. His wife's tomb is on the right. She was Doña Leonor, daughter of king Pedro IV of Aragón.

A statue to commemorate Juan II, showing him at prayer, is on the wall next to the tomb of queen Doña Juana Manuel.

This completes the series of six kings and three queens of Castile and Castile and Leon who are buried in Toledo cathedral.

THE RELIQUARY OR OCTAGON

This beautiful eight - sided room is behind the Chapel of the Virgin of the Sanctuary. It was designed and constructed by the famous architects Vergara and the son of El Greco, Jorge Manuel Theotocopoulos.

This room holds the cathedral's magnificent collection of relics. The 126 pieces of gold and silver work were made from the 13th to the 18th centuries.

The model of the four corners of the earth is also on display. This work dates from the 17th century, and shows the then known world. It is an Italian work, and was a gift from the widow of king Carlos II, Doña Mariana de Neoburgo. They are made of silver, and a different type of precious stone adorns each one.

The walls and ceiling are covered by frescos by Maella, Ricci and Carreño.

Vault: the octagonal room

84 *Reliquary chapel or Octagon*

THE OLD TREASURY HOUSE

Together with the Kress Foundation of the United States, and under the auspices of archbishop González Martín, the cathedral chapter inaugurated a series of new rooms in 1984. These are located in the Treasury House, a building beside the cathedral. It was built during the 16th and 17th centuries.

The rooms contain paintings by Caravaggio, Gerardo David and Sebastian del Piombo, together with sketches for the frescos by Bayeu and Maella on the cloister walls.

El Greco's sculpture of the investment of St Ildefonso is also on display here. This is the only remaining part of the old altar piece which used to hold the Spoliation.

St. John the Baptist: Caravaggio

THE CLOISTERS AND CHAPEL OF St BLAS

As most of the cloisters are closed off they are included in this appendix. However, on entering or leaving the cathedral one passes through the only side of them that is open to the public.

No cloisters were planned originally, due to lack of space. Nevertheless, archbishop Tenorio, who undertook many civil engineering works, ordered them to be constructed at the end of the 14th century. The market next to the cathedral was purchased for this purpose from the Jewish community. The construction of the upper cloisters started in 1500.

The arches of the lower cloister are topped by 18th century iron railings. These were designed by Basque blacksmiths, the Aldecoa brothers. The walls of the cloisters are covered by frescos, which are the work of Bayeu and Maella. They are also 18th century.

The entrance to the Chapel of St Blas is in one corner of the cloisters. This is where the founder of the cloisters, archbishop Tenorio, is buried. It contains a set of 14th century paintings. This is the most important example of these in Toledo, although some have been lost. Next to the tomb of the founder is that of his chaplain, Vicente Arias de Balboa. He was later Bishop of Plasencia.

We finish our walk around one of the most outstanding cathedrals in Europe here.

The Chapel of St. Blas

Photo : C. Casiano Alguacil

Photo : C. Casiano Alguacil

The perimeter walls of the Cathedral are crodwed in by nearby buildings, except around the main frontage.

The Cathedral with the bell tower of the old clock (demolished in 1888) stands out against a background of the flat walls of the enclosed convents and the unique geometrical forms of the roofs on the hillside. The Alcazar can be seen in the rear of the picture, as it was before it suffered the massive fire which completely destroyed it a year later.

90 *Santa Isabel street*

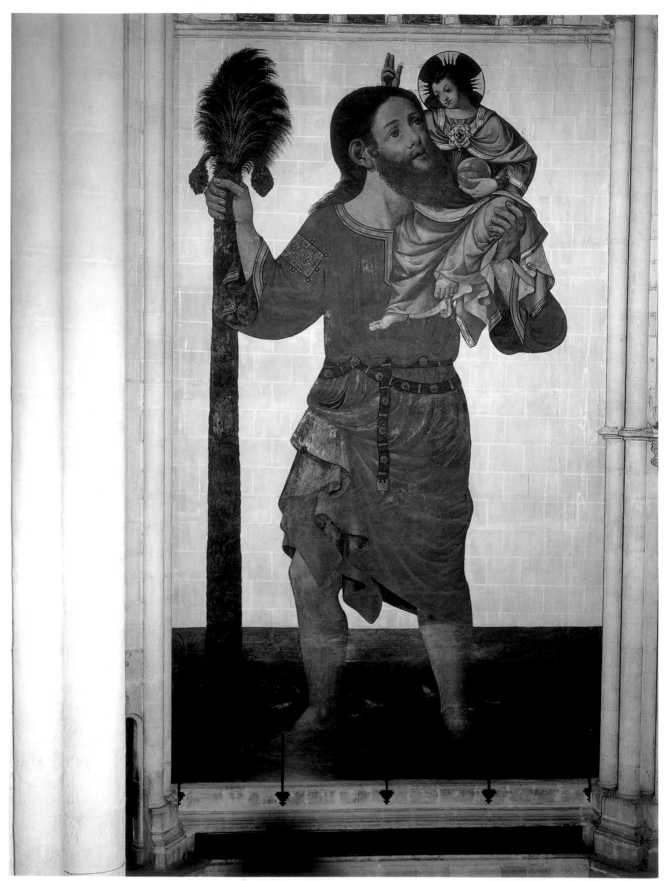

Saint Cristopher

GENERAL INDEX

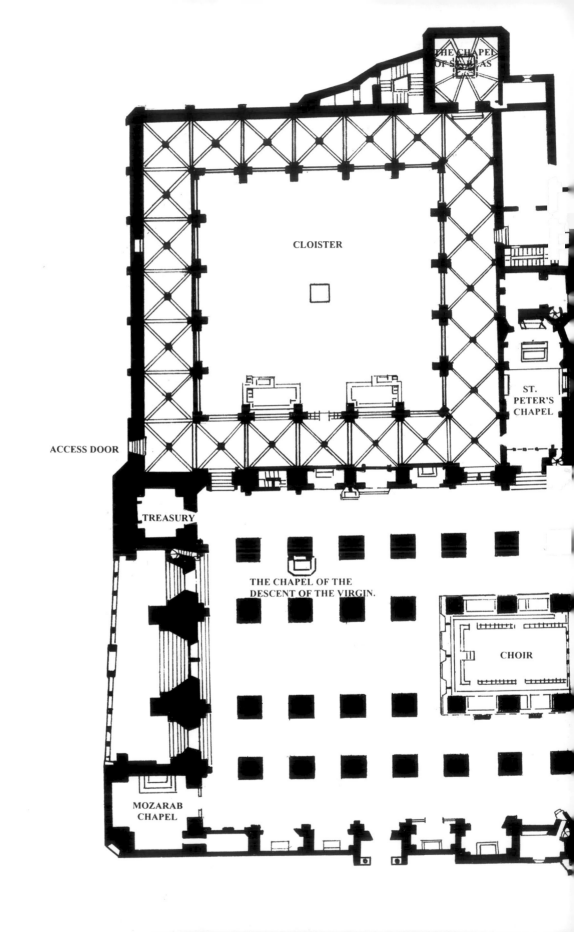

THE CHAPEL OF ST. LUKAS

CLOISTER

ST. PETER'S CHAPEL

ACCESS DOOR

TREASURY

THE CHAPEL OF THE
DESCENT OF THE VIRGIN.

CHOIR

MOZARAB
CHAPEL

PLAN OF THE CATHEDRAL

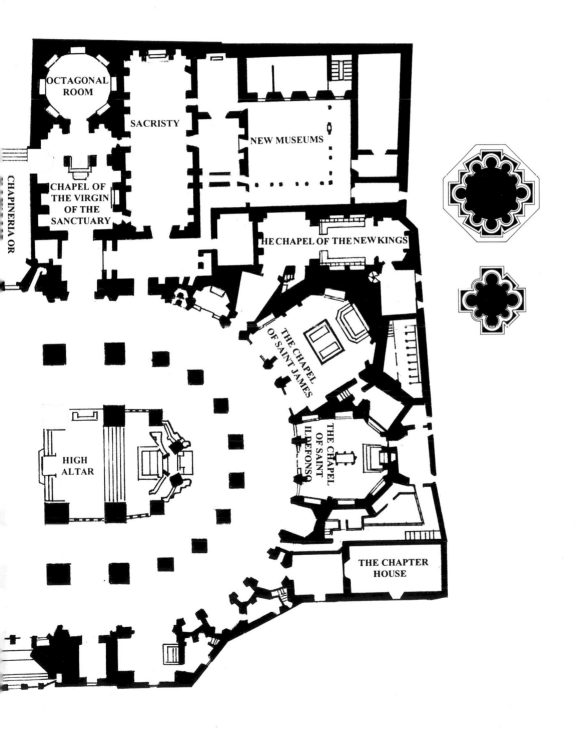

OCTAGONAL ROOM

SACRISTY

NEW MUSEUMS

CHAPINERIA OR

CHAPEL OF THE VIRGIN OF THE SANCTUARY

THE CHAPEL OF THE NEW KINGS

THE CHAPEL OF SAINT JAMES

THE CHAPEL OF SAINT ILDEFONSO

HIGH ALTAR

THE CHAPTER HOUSE